She Hath Cried

The Rebirth

By Queen NaAsia

Second Edition

2014

Per-Ankh Publishing Presents:

Edited by, Gwendolyn P. Jiles, M.Ed.

Why I Wrote This Book.

My five year old son, Shaatir, who is now seventeen, said to me:

"Mama, I know how God made the Sun."

"How baby?" I asked.

"He drew a picture, and he put it in the sky."

So, wrote this book.

Thank you, Muzikk Fenn for contributing to this project by designing the Cover Art.

Dedicated to the "Best Part", the babies.

Dear Reader,

At the onset, allow me to state, this is not a male-bashing book, rather a book which embraces the one eternal heart of all original spirits through a woman's mind, thus from a woman's perspective. I write to share these words, not to alienate anyone, rather to unify through common experience. My exploration of emotions is just that, a tour. The sentiments are not all mine, rather feelings I have found that one may experience, given certain circumstances. The opinions expressed are not all mine, but they are opinions, perspectives and philosophies I have had the pleasure or pain of being exposed to in my quest for truth. These truths, which eventually add up to the fact that there is a lie within every truth and truth embedded is embedded in every lie. These polarities transcend at the equator of your interpretation, your prime meridian being your own personal revelations, which are a tap away.

Therefore, it is not my intention to change your thinking in any way on any subject, but to widen your perspective and give you more options. My truest desire is that you might smile, laugh, remember, frown, disagree, or even cry, and that you may experience happiness, pleasure, anger, wrath, or even a moment of peace, but whatever the response, let it be yours. Come what may, my most sincere request is that this reading brings you more in tune with the universal spirit that all people share regardless of whom or what.

Peace,

Queen NaAsia

SHE HATH CRIED

A Collection of Original Poetry

by Queen NaAsia

"C'Mere Wench."

My journey, in this wilderness of North America, began on a Southern plantation, where I was a chocolate, slave-girl with wondering bright eyes. Eyes that glimmered with glee and excitement; amazement. I was bewildered by life, yet I remained docile, this being my way. Knowing nothing of tragedy and injustice, I assumed my circumstances were my due portion, and for this portion, I found love. It is the most inherent trait of a child to believe what it sees is the only existing reality, so reality for me was a rocking chair that squeaked beneath a roof of continuous leaks. Completely, I adored my mother's fatigued Sunday slumbers. My love for her was eclipsed only by my love for the seemingly never-ending cotton fields. Nature, its beauty, eclipses the most dark of despair. Rain, it seems to cleanse the most dingy of injustices, while the Sun beams its soothing rays with the sincerest equality known to man.

Eventually, I grew to love the thornish prick of a life that was so unlike my own, while mist the four gray walls that made my own shack. Within my own reach even. I cleaned there, played there, and on a good day, even ate there, but I could never live there. I was grateful to see the fine, wooden staircase, and the huge pictures of flowers and trees. The grand, cherry-oak piano, with its big white keys and little black keys. I touched it before. Good food and pretty plates, huge roasted ham and fruit. The vases, the walls had flowers....How I loved to clean, wash, brush and serve. Above all, I loved my master, God in person! I saw his picture in a book one day; his head was surrounded by the Sun.

He wore a purple, velvet robe, a score of Lambs about his feet. I was one of those lambs; I was at his feet. I longed to hear him say those words to me just one time.

"C'Mere Wench", he'd say, rarely, but verily, when he'd come at night for my mother. Reluctantly, she'd obey. I understood her all too well, her hesitance. I too, would probably quake with fear to so often be in such a close proximity to God; alone with God. He was such a powerful, feared and revered God, with pale, blue eyes that bore the reflection of the heaven. The entire of my world, his plantation bowed to him devoutly, and I do believe I was his most sincere subject. My mother always said: "Without God, where would we be?" 'Hell', I always thought. I saw the men from the plantation who would wander blindly off of the plantation, only to come back beaten and bloody. The world outside of the realm of our God must be grotesque indeed. Sometimes those men would not walk again, and some died, and were never seen again.

What heaven lied within those words? "C'Mere Wench!"? What majestical, wonderful place? I visioned paradise as I watched them part from the rest of us, him leading proudly, she following dutifully. As peculiar as it was us, she seemed to fret her partakings with his highness. She must have been overwhelmed with the pleasure of it all. Still, I was that wench, who longed to C'Mere. In vain, therefore, I awaited the day he'd come for me and take me off of the cotton field, just he and I, alone, freeing me of my chores and granting me my blissful portion. So much, I longed for this excursion; I decided to see for myself what raptures awaited me.

The merciless invasion of my fortress of gullibility and the security of my innocence were stolen away as thoroughly as they had afore been granted. As I assume Eve felt when she finally bit into that God forsaken, beckoning apple. As taunted, as tempted as she, seeking heaven first hand, I succumbed to the knowledge of bliss, the fallacious beckon of the serpent. I would see what pleasures embraced my fair mother, I would see heaven. My eyes salivated as does a hungry mouth about to be fed, and my tears streamed in starving expectation, when I crept behind them into our shack that day. She, her eyes filled with the most unusual joy I'd ever seen, lied down, exhausted on her and my father's bed. My father, at one time, gave her some pleasures in that bed. I heard them laugh, play and utter moans of joy on that very same bed, until God saw fit to take him away. My father being such a good man, God probably saw fit to send him to heaven right away, before the rest of us. To my dismay she raised her garments and spread the black hole, from which I had come, before my master, in a relenting agony. Before I could digest this, and as my eyes gapped wide, which was now being fed, my master, God, unfastened his pants, withdrew his white serpent, mounted my mother, and rammed the sharp blade of himself deep within her ungiving depth. She and he, now juxtaposed, had become one frictioning being. The power of his surges, the response of her defenseless retreat, the sourest of apples indeed. A worm surely lived in the apple I had bitten. I assume, as did Eve, I longed to spit this bitter, deceitful apple from my mouth. Yet, like her, gentle Eve, I could not turn back. Its venom was forever given leave to flow within the veins of my mental membrane and I would never be able to eject this

most unwelcome of truths from my blood.

I did squeeze my eyes shut to block the vision of this rape, from my eyes, but the unyielding beam of truth, the cries of my mother's and my hell pierced through my ears, exposing itself still. Each thrust and its yelp, yowl or whimper sent the pain of its violation within even my own tiny womb, with a towering assault, so much, it felt I might bleed. Distraught, I fled from our shack. Full of fury, betrayed, I ran toward the cotton field. Liar! Liar! Nature is a liar! I turned to the 'big house', what a beautifully disguised lie it was.

My gentle mother? Me? Your fatal trespass has rendered knowledge where there was question, wisdom where there was a mystery. You have lied on all your heavenly pretentions, and I have thus decreed that you are not God, in fact you are Satan. Your servants, demons, wife and all.

Cried at the thought of it all. Died at the sight of it all. These tunnels were not his. Now I trust nothing. I hate those white walls. Scrub I or not, there home is the blackest of blacks yet mist those deceiving whites. I ran for the outhouse and I squatted on the bucket to urinate, but when I looked in the bucket, it was overflowing with my blood. The blood of me, my mother, and her mother, and all the synonymous mothers spread about this wilderness of North America. Fainted from it all..

Years later, it was my turn. I was well prepared and endured it well. For, if my mother could endure it, gentle her, loving and caring her, I certainly could. My deepest fret by this time was that pain I of the inevitability of what lied before the fate of my own chubby, chocolate baby girl, Princess. All of her life, I knew it would happen to her, but I could never voice the words that would prepare her for her portion of the sour apple, which Eve and I shared. So I gave her love for preparation. Every biscuit, whisper, hug, cookie, or nibble of ham I gave her, was padding for the acidic apple she'd one day taste.

I felt her presence the day she could no longer wait to see where our master, the devil, took me. For some strange reason, I screamed louder that day. I knew she was biting the apple and I wanted it to be extremely sour; so sour that she could not stand the sight and flee as I did. I screamed, bowled, and yelped..."It Hurts.." not so much for me, but for my baby girl, Eve, as the devil raped my nation through me, my daughter, my mother, thus we, simultaneously. As I folded the padding for her undergarments to catch the trickling spills of womanhood, I avoided the dimness from her once bright eyes. I knew why she stared at me so tenderly now; she adored me and pitied me at the same time. As I'd worshipped and mourned my own mother, now passed. For my beloved baby girl, whose elegance and regality waited to be invaded by the venomous milk that tormented all, I had no defense. I had nothing to protect her from the secret torture now exposed.

So together she and I, my mother and me, we faced the world, the hell of it. The unfairness of this labyrinth. Our plights became so congruent that we became a league of sisters. Hand and hand, generation after generation, we brushed her stringy hair,

and oiled the feet of the devil's wife. We used our fatigued hands to massage her rested feet, at her whim. Luxuriated her, fed her babies from my own bosom; however we could never wash away the filth of her atrocities nor the singe of her dismay. Dismayed, because even as I massaged, rubbed, and caressed, we communicated telepathically and I read the truth of her and my realities. She bowed in awe, envying the power of I, whose ray of fire was such from my eyes that I assaulted her soul with my very glare. The treasure within the realm of me, which her husband craved irrationally, she hated that craving which she could not satiate. Not even the gyration chore, with which she charged my husband, could equate her to me. For in me lied the heaven of both ebony and ivory.

Me, the beautiful, the radiant flower seemed to spawn from the grimiest mud, while she, so fertilized, so well kept, remained but a weed in both of their eyes. The truth of it all, my divinity, descended to this great dishonest abyss, where she could even fathom being my superior, quickened her so, though she had no recourse, but to exalt me and dethrone me at the same time. I survived these chronicles completely and utterly insane. I found my only pleasure was giving, receiving nothing but requital or approval from what I disperse from my own self. That ray of fire that was once my eyes has calmed to a smoldering river, which has produced a global warming in me. I have embraced my translucent fate. That was and is yet the entirety of my span, my ever present, blood-soaked portion. Fed because I feed, loved, because I love, seen because I see. It all comes back to me......Some things never change

Remembrance

I call forth to your remembrance, the whips, the chains, the pains.

No blood stains, because clothes weren't fit for my people.

There was no equal, we were the lowest of the low.

We had nowhere to go, just seeds to sow.

And even though we emerged victorious, claiming victory

It's getting to me, because I feel we

Need to be called to remembrance.

Reminiscence on 400 years of tragedy

Embraced by his sympathy, majesty, his apathy.

Still we choose to release the belief

in the source that brought forth true relief.

Seeking not to dwell on, but to flee

memories that assault us.

Casting the past in a turbulent sea of a new found misery,

which we, have allowed to be manifested.

Broken hearted, congested.

They've confessed, not suppressed it, still we detest it.

Seek Remembrance.

I call forth to your memory, auction blocks, shiny grease.

No peace, no sleep, little to eat; nowhere to creep.

Only belief in better ways, hope for better days.

Pride for runaway and fear castaways.

Slaves, property, prisoners with no listeners.

No one heard us, we were murdered; they were murderers.

Killed at will, not allowed but one skill.

Not permitted to take a pill, with no cut on the deal.

Stripped of dignity, still we

Need remembrance.

I'm calling to your cipher a Queen

dehumanized, beaten and raped.

Fallen from her rightful place, agony on her blessed face.

Enemies in her precious space.

Her beautiful bosoms his dark tongue did taste.

Her womb ramp sacked,

with no hope of gaining its sacredness back.

Her uterus interrupted, vagina flooded.

I shudder as I utter these soliloquies

of Hell on Earth but first..

I need your remembrance.

Strong and prouder than a Lion, King manifested immortal.

His shoulders spanned wide like an eagle, with no equal

Captured, whipped and chained by white people.

No sequel can ever compete with this tornado spun.

Supreme violation of this magnificent one.

And no reefer can ever bring back the fresh

No cocaine can replace the flesh.

No alcohol suppress the pain that's in his chest.

Although he was blessed,

This is the test of all tests.

This mess stripped the bird from the nest.

The contest is in you, it's true.

You can do what you wanna do,

but just remember, that Black December,

That Cold November.

The burning timber.

Our Nation's dismember.

The Pot Yet Simmers.

We were all members of this painful holocaust.

The great lost,

This True and Living Memory..

..Let us remember...

...Lest we forget.

What's In The New?

Why do your headlines equal dead minds and land mines?

Why do you say I spread crimes and coke lines, when I write rhymes?

This just in.

Some more of my kin have been executed.

After being hoodwinked, bamboozled and prostituted.

How is it you hold our lives at your whim?

Four hours before execution, appeal denied, Kill him!

Shameless lies, you utter from your lips, still no one trips.

You broadcast slave auctions and burnt church clips.

Cast eyes down I hate the sound of this continuous.

Another black man slain, no evidence, no witnesses.

No testimony no search party ignited.

No moment of silence, these remarks..I flip the script and rewrite it.

Today's headlines read, indeed, our hearts bled.

Blood runs red, frustrated, agitated and misled; misfed.

Rendering us dehydrated, with malnutrition.

Enveloped in superstition, seeking a mystery petrified of a

revolution.

Beneath a constitution, clearly deeming I as three fifths.

Yet I roll blunts, pull stunts, twist caps, take sips.

Although with each swig I drink, I neglect to think.

That I am consuming my own blood, making my people extinct.

So what's in the news??? Interludes

of brainwash, religion, as my race concludes.

All of a sudden, it's no secret

They speak it, teach it, and even preach it:

Our demise.

Penal plantations overcrowded, closed third eyes.

Black gold is abundant, your taxes fund it.

Your overseer is the warden, rather or not you done it.

So tell me how we run it: Exactly as we were taught.

Their tutelage is impressive these things, robbery, rape and larceny.

Let's examine the record.

Upon theft of an occupied land, the colored man took and stated:

"Behold, this maze I orchestrated."

Using rape as a tool, diluted Allah's schools.

Kidnapping millions remorseless killings

rampant blood spillings.

Committed ride-bys from slave ships.

Came equipped with trick gifts:

Fabric, Guns and Wine,

shiesty devil lying.

Conspiracy to commit suicide, unveil the documents.

Klan land, Super Man; look at the government.

This damned, doomed nation

is on one hell of a probation.

...The News.

......and then there was Columbine..

The Blood Ran Red

Thirteen senseless killings in a state of no risk.

Whole life splattered on a blank, lazer disk.

Random hearts ceased beating, while the school reeked with fear.

After committing a million murders, they said: "Let us out of here!"

Society frowns on the boys with a thousand rounds.

Armed to the teeth: "We must blow the school down!"

The country appalled at this strange twist of fate.

What only happens in the ghetto, has proclaimed a new trait.

Swat teams and lazer beams, hesitating to diffuse the scene

Although it seems that had it been me and mine

they would have blown the school up; it would have been just fine.

Pipe bombs and tanks of propane came to disdain

this state of democracy that they proclaim.

They weren't insane, they were creative.

Now look at the legislative

trying to make sense of this, trying to repent for this,

with no care or concern for the blood my brothers spent before this.

Assaulted by the precedent, my patience spent.

When I heard of the incident, I went: "Somebody issue a reprint."

The government produced this tangent.

Spent on a life of black grief,

because our babies cry and barely eat.

You should shrink when you see me.

I thought my people were supposed to be

the number one public enemy.

Can you feel me?

All I know is fourteen kids and a man are dead,

And the coroner's report said the blood ran red.

Let our souls respond to this turbulent dawn

of mankind at his finest still dwelling in blindness.

Unkindness to those like me, who live inner-city,

With no daddy, a Future cd, no vision, but destiny.

The president will never visit the funerals in my hometown.

Therefore his hypocrisy is eradicated.

The trench coat mafia laid it down.

Let us reflect, as our hearts respond, let us reflect.

America gets no respect.

So now when you dwell in your daily travelings and see single, white men,

Grab your purse and clutch your head and watch their heads spin.

Maybe then they'll see how it feels,

Because they are the authors of the book that kills.

Yet and still I couldn't help but smile

to see for once, it wasn't a black child..

Justice on the horizon, balance in a little while.

But Honey, child, they have some explaining to do now.

Why did a privileged intellectual seek to make his teacher bow?

What do you expect, when the president can bring

a whore to the White House and the secret service won't sing?

Don't blame it on Ms. Tripp, the president slipped.

He had a precious gem on his hip.

I guess not precious enough to make him stay.

Poor example for my brothers with his savage, wicked ways.

All I can say is fourteen kids and a man are dead.

And the coroner's report said the blood ran red.

The blood ran red, my people, not blue or brown.

Wasn't caramel or chocolate and it wasn't watered down.

May peace and blessings be on the minister, because Malcolm laid it down.

The roosters have come home to roost in this town.

Although you may not wanna hear it, because most of us fear it.

The Wrath of God is on America and the apocalypse, we are getting near it.

Check your spirit and embrace your kids.

Tell them look at the news, see what our captors did.

You are not inferior! You are a manifested black, over-achiever in overachiever in the making.

Lift your head and straighten your shoulders, and leave your adversaries quaking.

Let's make lies of these liars, ignite our mental fires.

Every dog has his day and so this tragedy transpired.

It reminds us that the universe sees no skin color.

Every nation will kill his brother, in the masses.

Psychotic devil and his madness.

Limits are being broken daily, you can ace those classes.

You can obtain whatever you desire.

Don't let anybody tell you different!

Mathematical, Logical, Kinesthetic-Linguistic.

All I know is fourteen kids and a man are dead.

And the coroner's report said: "The Blood Ran Red".

They

They locked him away from me.

Shackled him and chained him to where we couldn't see.

No sympathy, won't emphasize, but continue to criticize

The rhythm and the rhyme of which black people live their lives.

Implemented a chaotic society, then policed it.

Trained and angered a ferocious dog and released it

on me and my babies, and now castration is the answer.

Incarcerate their future; cure this criminalistic cancer.

Unwillfully injected, are our brothers, with hatred and turmoil.

The ghetto has them spoiled.

Simply put, fertile seeds die in contaminated soil.

While we toil and we tally, they have Democratic rallies.

Republican parties vs. drug deals in the alley.

We hesitate to communicate, mate because our souls are stuck and debate

The outcome of the neonate our chromosomes will create.

The heart of the ghetto must portray a better way.

For as we slay, we must remember, it wasn't us, it was they.

It was they, they, them, and those who chose

to call us Negroes, bitches and hoes.

We are shocked and froze, but suppose

we revamp this modern day boot camp,

which ships our brothers and sisters off to get stamped.

On their pants, on their shirts, jail ids.

Born Enemies.

Ingenuity is needed to change times like these.

To cool eyes like these.

They've turned Kings into thieves.

Naturals to weaves, yet I still believe

that through righteousness we can retrieve

and upon completion conceive a new nation of Princes and

Princesses who will never leave.

When I am reminded of a holding cell, I try to think well.

He should be in jail for a crack cocaine sell.

But when I ask him where forth did it grow; He tells me he doesn't know

The true origination of this priceless snow.

Once again bamboozled, led astray; betrayed.

In the terms of the streets, the boy got played.

Check the circumstances, hungry people take hungry chances.

Just as negativity leaves the mind as the soul enhances.

Sent off by millions to new plantations.

Abandoning 3 to 5 baby mamas to a cruel organization.

With no patience, death chasing.

Their children aren't unharmed, their mothers are not armed.

So Clinton puts his signature on the Welfare Reform.

Young mothers in awe and he tells them, deal with it.

A 4.5 on the Richter, the knife is in and it's twisted.

Death is the goal, genocide is the destination.

Don't trust this nation.

It was they.

The constitution was magnificent; they wrote it and signed it.

Lied on it a million times, till the country was blinded.

Rewind it back to a time when we grew up in peace.

In our own communities, where we had no beef.

We mobilized united we got things done.

And at times it seemed like the war was won.

But then came guns that shoot a million times.

Got brothers and sisters hooked on crack, like they were once hooked on wine.

I ain't lying.

If you with me, put a finger up, if you're against me,

You disagree, put two fingers up.

Cause they've got you souped up.

That's why you scream Peace!

Though your brother's deceased.

It's about time busy, high time to get political.

Of a country that kills my people, I am highly critical.

I'm expelling every disbelief that our brothers aren't fit

To rule a home, be great fathers, and have pure spirits.

But if it's up to the other, this dark nation that crucifies my brothers.

Not each other..shall they not incarcerate another.

My people unite till we imperfect the way

They continuously send us to dismal dooms days.

It was they.

"Check Yes or No"

The years later, poverty-ridden. I remember the holes in my garment, which were like the passages through which I was assaulted by my peers. They taunted me reminding me of the things I didn't have, suggesting that maybe I shouldn't laugh at the jokes that were being told, because maybe my shoes were so old. Or at least don't laugh too loud, before someone would break my smile and say:

"NaAsia whatchu laughing at with them big ole holes in your shoes? You be quiet! Before I go get a chocolate milk and pour it in that thirsty curl of yours!"

Back into my cave I crawled. Hear no evil see no evil and surely speak it not. I was content with the idea that this would be the Christmas when I'd get two pairs of shoes enough outfits for an entire week, and maybe...an atari.

To this day, I am still amazed that some of my classmates' parents had enough money to buy them shoes that matched their clothes, and give them spending money every day. I can close my eyes now and see the Red Hot Riplets, grape Now 'n Laters and orange Vess sodas; the yellow blouse which matched the yellow seam of their Levi jeans. I remain bewildered.

Don't ask me how it happened, but somehow, on God's Green Earth, Anthony saw beyond all that. One sunny day, shoes with holes, thirsty curl and all, Anthony found me beautiful and sent me a note by Randy, my Aunt Candy's baby's daddy sister's oldest daughter's best friend. It read:

I like you. Do you like me???

Check Yes__ or No__

I never answered back. It had to be a joke, but not knowing held so many possibilities. It meant that maybe not having shoes to match your outfit didn't matter. Maybe having holes in your shoes was something that, at the tender age of twelve, was out of my control. It meant freedom, freedom to dream, freedom dare; freedom to change. It meant that maybe your sons and your daughters would one day have many outfits and that you could give them spending money, everyday..and that all would be well.

It's Mine

It's mine, why should I give it away??

He's lying how can that make him stay??

I know I'm right, he's not my husband.

What's wrong with getting to know my mind?

I think I can teach him something.

He was mad when he left, so he couldn't have been honest.

I bet he won't even call like he promised.

Well if he doesn't, It won't hurt me none.

I have the respect I had before and then some.

I think too highly of myself to spread thin.

My soul mate won't go behind a hundred men.

If he really thought anything of himself

he'd be glad I wasn't giving it to him or anyone else.

I think being a virgin can be a good thing.

One thing I know for sure is what casual sex can bring.

I could've let him touch me. It probably wouldn't have hurt.

What if he really doesn't call me when he gets home from work??

Everybody says it feels good they say they can't live without it.

Well, I've been without it my whole lifetime and so I tend to doubt it.

I guess I better go with my first mind,

because once it's done, you can't rewind.

And if I don't hear from him again,

I'll join a chess club and meet some other young men.

Teacher Flows Her Woes

Tormented, Daily I die,

It kills me inside.

Yesterday I almost cried.

I almost cried yesterday. In fact, the pools did fill my eyes.

Yet I blinked them away in a senseless pride.

Priceless tides of sadness consumed me, as my student sat in the room with me,

Sorta like a cartoon to me, I wondered what their dooms would be.

Tragedy, its reality, in my supreme regality

I am forced to witness my nation's fatality.

Its scene was like that of Ethiopia, on the TV screen,

open to flies, which surround them.

Ignorance drowning them, day after day, I try to resound them.

Motivated, I enter this dragon with all my might

Striving, with all my vigor, to make this wrong right.

There was a time when knowledge was kept in a sacred college.

To study or read, we'd stowe away in a closet.

Though time has passed, the struggle still remains

Waiting to be born from this generation's brains.

That intensity, the propensity that freed us still needs us.

The scraps and beatings, the rape still bleed,

but somewhere in this succession of years, bloodshed and tears

turned to thugs, death and fear.

Have you ever wanted something so much

that when you receive it, it seemed a sin to touch?

The person, who had it, dangled it before you, literally whipped you with it.

Though you witness it, when I present it, you resent it.

It's documented, we hyper-vented, truth showers.

There's no sphinx nor secret cult to this, knowledge is power.

So will the power of this knowledge, your lips ever know?

Or will this nonsense continue to be our flow, as our people die slow?

It haunts me, taunts me, it kills me inside.

Yesterday I almost Cried.

I almost cried when I looked in those beautiful, brown eyes

to see traces of your lies, the masks, behind which you hide.

Entering your nursery, to share with you my vision.

Instead I see you suffering from malnutrition.

So slim it scares me, staring there at me
Was a starving infant wearing misery.
So skinny, I see the flesh through your bones.
Angry, because I bug you and won't leave you alone.
Cursing, kicking and spitting.
Rebelling, lashing and hitting.
Quitting before you finish.
Afraid to be another failure's witness.
I'm here every day with the very same food.
You refuse it, jam your mouth shut, you're rude.
Every day I come back, same food; same story.
Few successes, little progress, no happiness; no glory.
Yesterday I came and looked; you were so sickly, wow!
I have to feed this dying child; I have to save him now.
Yet each night I return home with the delicious food I've prepared,
containers still flowing with sustenance, little I have shared.
Thinking to myself, asking myself am I crazy.
Yet I'll continue to do this daily.
I have faith in the babies.

"Pssst, Can I Get Your Number??"

...I live in the Matrix. I wake up and go to school, come home and do my homework and my choirs. I cook, babysit, watch TV, bathe and sleep, constantly. No one pays me attention. No one knows I'm alive. I am forever plugged.

The thought that I could actually get attention from young men, because I wore tight, blue jeans blew my mind. Especially since the tight jeans weren't my choice, but only resort. I hear the shouts, horns blowing and the infamous:

"Pssst....Can I get your number??"

....You most certainly can. Call me two or three times and you can get in my pants. I'll skip school for you, respect and obey only rules made by you. Why? Because no one has paid me this much attention in years. I skip school, and disobey my mama without fear. Just to hear those three little words: "I love you". Or even two: "You fine!". Your acceptance of little ole me, renders me blind.

By the way does that really feel that good? Can I truly produce magic like that? Do you find me that beautiful, youthful and truthful? ...

"..Of course, I love you. You and only you..."

"That's good, baby...I wanted to tell you that I missed my period this month. I know how much you love me and how good I make you feel, and I know we'll make a happy family.

..Don't stress it. You could get a job at McDonald's and with my welfare check, we could...

.........What you mean, it ain't yours??? I haven't been with anyone but you!!!

IT IS YOURS!!!!??

Hello??

....Hello???

......HELL-LO???!!!!.."

(Operator's Voice) "I'm sorry, you seemed to have reached womanhood. There's no one here to take your call. Please check the number or try your call again-and, yes little sister: Hell is Low."

Depthless

Irrationally, we disagree, usually about God's identity.

When he, eternally, systematically dwells within you and me.

Obviously, it's a conspiracy.

Rhetorically, it's hypocrisy.

This is not a matter of discussion.

Rampant combustions of sudden

disagreement causes expedient

transfusions of confusion.

The illusions are protruding

through the magnificence.

Irrelevance is repelling the iridescence.

Inevitably, we bicker.

Quick to say the next one is sicker.

When apparently

there are so many similarities.

Evidently, it's not a coincidence.

Apparently, it's fake confidence.

Let he who has achieved perfection, make the selection

and commence with the ejection of those we will despise.

Cast down our eyes.

Their demise will be expedient.

Their death a truculent determinant.

Let us heinously expel their dwell.

Then dissipate them to an eternal hell.

But, oh well, he without flaw, exists not.

So let's sort through the morass of this elaborate plot.

Constantly, we declare divinity,

supremacy over colleagues in life.

Claiming to be conquerors of all the strife.

...right.

The incongruity of prosperity,

The inconsistency of felicity.

Auspicious, suspicious irregularities

of subordinate polarities.

How frequent are these

transparencies.

Things of tangibility

based not on individuality.

Logically the mentality, which mentally tallies

must factor in abnormalities,

and circumstances of limited chances.

So often miscalculated, it's been stated, since recent studies show.

The value of most treasure diminishes the deeper in the abyss you go.

...you know?

Unclaimed Property

As I glare up at you through tiny slits that are barely open

Somewhere within that smile of yours, I perceive that you are hoping

my silky hair remains fine, my pupils fails to define, to the father who is blind

that the fact is, I'm not his, and the truth is that you're lying

on my genetic makeup, the optimum betrayal.

The loving mother, faithful wife, yes fallacious portrayal

of life, built upon my innocence.

With no repentance, you seek, and pray my appearance

doesn't bear witness, remains a facade on a soul that doesn't speak.

To each spirit in heaven awaiting birth my heart wreaks.

Shall they not be the victim of this most blemishing deceit.

Born to a lie, destined to die a sad death.

Sentenced to a life of appraisal from my very first breath.

See, he doesn't know me, his semen never made my acquaintance.

Now, after nine months of curiosity, enveloped in patience.

I am appalled to see that question in your face; that fear in your eyes.

That anxiety, that apprehension of a mother, who lies.

Oh, woe, woe..woe is me.

This fatherless child, this unclaimed property.

"Where Yo Man At?"

If she pours water on me one more time.....She thinks that just because she babysits for me, she can run me. Why I need a diploma anyway? I'm sick of giving her half of my welfare check. My baby needs things. I want the new Jordans. I should get my own place. I'll put an application in for public housing. Toya say her rent is just $13. Plus she gets $300 in food stamps. She be having her whole check. Then I can quit going to school and watch Ricki Lake, Jenny Jones, and Jerry Springer, eat cheesecake, and do my hair. Man first chance I get, I'm out of there....

Those were my thoughts as I stood on the bus stop, in the middle of December, wishing someone would free me from mama's jail.

Plus it's cold out here!

When out of the clouds of heaven, my angel, Rodney appeared. Curl hanging and breath stankin' from menthol t-shirt, Reeboks, starched Levis, six-feet tall. His four words changed it all:

"Where Yo Man At???"

"My man..." I retorted with spunk, "is a non-existent entity of false hopes, pipe dreams, and chaos at its highest realm. Now can you retrieve she who grieves by fulfilling all her needs?

He turned and squinted at me.

Into his yellow-rose smelling Buick Century I leapt,

ignoring the vapor of alcohol and marijuana chasers.

Hush now, Mama. Keep the welfare check. This man is putting gold around my neck. The crack heads and dealers, now, give me respect. Now I know how it feels to fold and stack money. Matter of fact, the diploma's yours, I finally got it. I'm in the dope game honey.

Say what, say hunh?? Please! He pays the rent at 1905 Palm and his loving is the bomb!? So if he is laying up with you too; you should be proud to give him some. That's how I'm seeing it. Rich, I'm being it, living it. Everything I ever wanted, he's giving it.

Sitting in my crib, sipping gin and juice picking my long nails, I receive the call. Rodney is in prison. That ends it all.

I wanna move back with my mama, but I disrespected her, so we don't talk. I wonder why everything she's said makes sooo much sense now????? hmmm...

Dirty Bra

I can't believe what I just saw.

That girl has on a dirty bra.

I must say that I am in awe

that she'd be seen with such a flaw.

I know I am not the only one who sees.

I bet her house is infested with fleas.

It's true that I am not really involved,

but with a little soap and water, that could have been solved.

Sometimes I really wonder what's wrong

with people who just wonder along...

With her trifling self, she needs to quit.

It's stuff like this that makes me sick.

That's why people say bad things about us

Like that we are nasty, lazy and all we do is cuss.

And you really can't blame 'em when a full grown woman..

Naw, forget all that.

I'ma teeellll her something!

"Um, Excuse me..

I WAS STANDING ACROSS THE ROOM OVER THERE...

...and I couldn't help noticing...

I mean, I don't mean to be rude, BUT!

Let me just say, that's a stunning beige bra you're wearing..

...my slip is showing???

Thank you, My sister."

..in retrospect..respect.

Opposition

Liar, my heart calls me as I encase it in glass.

Free me it cries..

It longs to know the sun's rays within its cells.

It accuses me of promoting its hell.

Its beating has accused me guilty

of rendering its lonely throb to an eternity of celibance.

It begs; it craves sustenance.

Yet, I refuse it, despite the signs of its starvation.

It is my soul's hate that I embark on this clandestine course,

but I cannot make my heart another empty promise.

See it, dearest one, this thing my heart, but pray do not touch it.

It, this cursed thing, as barren as the moon.

You see her inviting gleam, she beckons you..

but, pray...do not touch her.

Love, though gentle ointment, was a tortuous symphony.

Each chord of that feared enemy raped my soul,

Injecting its much denied venom into my mind.

Yet I danced to that assault completely and utterly and

at times I yet partake on its melodic battery.

Swaying within its monologue,

pretending to be alive, when I know that tune has ended.

I gyrated to that sunken ship and with each dip I took,

my heart shook..spasmed raged..accusing me.

Love was a delightful play.

See, my love O picture of perfection.

See it as it, as though if a maze, it draws you in, then abandons you.

Leaving you to find your own way out.

Know what it truly is before you enter.

Do see it, please,

but pray, do not touch it.

I do not agree with me.

I do not support what I have come to be.

I cannot uphold this lewd integrity

I am already a victim, awaiting the great larceny.

Commit that theft on me.

See my love, my heart, you must incarcerate it

against my will.

I shall not, I cannot give it, I have refused then to free it.

Don't.

Peace, is not my portion.

My cup doth not taste an ounce of it.

So that, peace, a thing I crave.

Thirstfully, I await its rivers come chasing me

yet I am guaranteed to flee from its soft currents.

Behold Peace, peace, I do see it..

But I will not touch it.

Bound in opposition of self.

Tasting breath, yet knowing every volume of death.

Back tracking my steps, snail-like, I crept, alone I wept.

Upon my path, hell is next.

Those lovers tried to wake me, shake me, still I slept.

I knew no one was hearing my prayers, still I knelt.

Longing to be an igloo, but what if I melt?
All I know is how abandonment felt.

I detest this cursed hand I was dealt.

Its cards of disappointment, regret, turmoil and tragedy.

I cannot change these cards to winners, yet I cannot resign from this game.

The psychic has conferred with the jinns and the verdicts in..

I cannot win.

She Hath Cried

She hath Cried too long.

She hath Cried too long.

Her only desire was his.

She hath Cried.

She hath witnessed murder.

Constant tears, but no one heard her...

..silent, rampant..tears.

Cries, screams, Cries..tears.

That pain that she hath beared..

Witness to the death of her children, their slaughter.

Her own son her cherished, beautiful daughter.

She hath held her wrath.

She cried.

Upon that flimsy thing, you call a shoulder,

you grew younger, she grew older.

Baptized in her own liquids.

Bathed in her own fluids.

Immortalized by her pain.

Divine, she were.

Angelic, art her.

Infalliable, she art.

Unselfish, her heart.

Pools, from her eyes.

Stains, from your lies.

Strength, her disguise.

Death, in her cries.

When will you realize?

That when she cries, your spirit cries with her.

You are the frame to her picture.

You are the vase of her bouquet.

You are the torch, light her way.

She Hath Cried..

She Hath Died..inside.

She hath Exalted.

She hath spread wings, this divine thing,

Such a beautiful being.

Your reflection cast down.

Her tears make no sounds.

Her soul bears the proof.

Her eyes tell no lies.

Her tattered dress.

Her dirty scarf.

Her run over shoes.

Her calluses, her corns, her wounds, her scars, her history..

in this labyrinth..this wilderness..

Her triumph..

Her promise..

She hath spread those wings.

She hath flown to the unknown...alone.

Join her.

INTERLUDE

ADULTEROUS SYMPHONY

"The Flutes"

Summon to Heaven

My heart is a godforsaken place. A place of condemnation and abominations. A desolate place, bursting with possibilities, hopes, fears, integrity, and rhetoric. With hidden passageways, vaults overflowing with jewels. Key holes, which unlock rivers of emotions, gates of hell, wrath even. There is a place in my heart, which you hold the exclusive key to. When you turn it, ever so gently, it releases a chamber of tranquility.

Thus, I have sat your naked body on its couch of freshly picked roses, peeled petal by petal, plucked free of thorns. I sit you there and pour out a delicate mixture of milk and honey for you to drink, while I play classical ballads, which caress and invoke your soul, infiltrating your mental, flowing simultaneously with your blood, upwards and downwards, sending electrical pulses up your spine till my love enters your brain, driving you insane. Causing you to feel and touch silk velvets softly caressing your face. Absorbing you, pulling you in so deep, deep into this chamber of calm.

It is my truest desire that you are inclined to lock that door. I covet you slamming that door, locking your and my entire selves in this magical place. To dwell therein infinitely, leaving all else to work itself out. I wish you could stay here. I need you to be here. Accompany me. I dream of you and I locking this place off, barricading the door with our love. Permitting the admittance of nothing unholy, nothing foreign.

In this space, my heart, I seek to avail you the opportunity to lay down the weight of your life; your sorrows, hopes and

aspirations. Tell me who hurt you, how, why. Wanting to provide you with such a beautiful feeling of resolution and bringing your life's business to such a beautiful close, reducing the deficits of your soul to a memory. What was, that is now, not. Square dealt. Emitting ciphers so stagnated on 360 that you'll become oblivious to the rotation, aware of Peace only, embracing its outcome so. In such room, I'd like to rig a film strip and lay you upon that said bed of roses only this time providing, for you, a private cloud to rest your head upon. Rest there, while I show you the scenes from my life:

A movie with no sequel, nor equal, and epic drama, satirical parody, sci-fi, mystery, comedic, action thriller. With scenes that will drain tears from your eyes like freshly sliced onions. Scenes so humorous, these onions prevail.Scenes so painful, so dark these onions yet prevail. Car crashes, drunken stupors, violence, oh well. I'd show you. I'll show you...flashbacks to a turbulent childhood. Things that didn't turn out like they should. Times I tried so hard to be good. Times when I promised I would, knew I could, and didn't.

Praying that after you see this Gothic horror, running aside a romantic hope-filled, skin-flick, you invite me to join you upon that couch and nestle me in your strong arms and gently kiss my tears away as I taste the salt from your tears mixed with my fears, our years. Alas, you lie back and the spreading out of your arms beckons me to ascend your mount and as you gently enter my dream catcher, rapture upon rapture. Building levels of understanding with the unspoken communication. So high, so high, so high. Traveling past galaxies, in this great space, my heart, I close mine eyes and all I see are celestial bodies and constellations. Heat, Warmth, Air; Earth, Wind, Fire. Rapidly we approach Heaven's Gate.

Behold! A knock at the door. So overwhelmed am I that I hardly hear it. You look in my tear filled eyes, questioning me. “Can you hear it?” Regretfully I do hear it. I hear it, as much as I despise it, I still hear it. Your and my eyes enter the dialogue. What shall we do? You know the vigor with which I want you. Shall I descend the most gallant; most thorough of all mounts I've ridden? Why? How? Not Now..

For you and I know what lies beyond that door...Reality, clothed in responsibility and accusation, riddled with insinuations and guilt. He and her, defined both. Our love ones, paths we subconsciously chose, or conscienceless for responsibilities sake. Pursuant to righteousness. When what can be brighter than this spread about heaven? Paradise tossed about. Reality is out there, at the door demanding, holding four cocoons in its palms, stating “Submit...submit to the verdicts of your own frivolous, uninformed decision.” Reality beats, ranting, “You owe me. You belong to me.”

I descended. Naked. Reluctantly. Hailing your majesty, clothing you with coat and arms, pushing you out of me covered with droplets of sweat. Vapors of love unplugged. I inspect your garments, searching for wrinkles, the slightest hint of unkemptness. Seeing none, I retreat, I hide as you unlock and exit the sanctuary of my heart with much hesitation. Do glance back.

Alone now, I resume the watching of the film. It has its good points, but I don't wanna die here. Reality left me two cocoons, but how can I nurture them? I have placed them in the warmest of places, but I can't take my eyes off of this sad movie. Only in your presence did I truly breathe.

I miss you.

When, who is reality to point its finger at me, condemning me, when I only sought to heaven my God. When I only sought to

bear your reflection with the grace and dignity it deserves. She couldn't do that. I despise her...I adore him..I admire her..I resent him. But you say this is not a labyrinth. I start to think of your pilgrimage and I wonder. What if he needs me? Who will console him? I carry his coat. I hold his umbrella. I long to chaperon you on this journey to provide you with shelter, but who will shelter me? Left alone with another episode, Innocence Lost. I want to surrender. I want to not care, but at what cost?

Chaotic Rapture

I call forth to you from another God's heaven. Why must I reverence you so? Are you my soul mate? The thought of you supersedes physical or mental engagement with any male entity manifested in this physical realm we call life. Do express to me what has commenced in my heart without my permission. Your divine intervention has produced chaos where there was once a thing that resembled peace. All around me, why was chaos my portion, before this order, thereby I have lived only to stumble upon this path, my love for you. Chaos yet again..Chaos Being.

Completely I long to free this damsel, who hath grown to be your Eternal Helpmeet. Her, your wife, willing dove, your servant. She, who beckons me in the transgressions of my love for you. She, who believes; trusts, because she knows. She, whom I have taunted, rendering her ignorant and irrational. She, abandoned, yet trusting. Stupid her. I want to be her. Only if you will be him that welcomes her. Extinguishing us, the fearful ones. These things, which we plan are indeed possible. It is of certainty, these things, mathematically precise, were written aforetime in the archaic scribes of the universe. It is of a surety, our forming molecules have waltzed.

Howbeit, we have but a Tale of Two Cities to render forth toward our heaven. No tales of us, we, in accordance. We must, we shall bring forth offerings to this, our paradise decreed. This utopia, kissing your lips, licking your spine. Promising a physical tour of this wisdom, she who is not fleeing. Us, bearing witness to you as God and I-Self as Earth. Before you pass from this physical realm, you shall taste the bliss of me. That your understanding eye does multiply with mine, that bond which, concealed or revealed, is due.

I know not of, nor care for these definitions; husband, wife, marriage, spouse; fidelity. These terms of imprisonment, which seek to confine me, while I am yet a slave to thee alone.

I, being her, aforementioned, who was incarcerated from the onset of this scribe, hence revolting against self, mine ego. She who would say, "I cannot love you." She who would swear, "I cannot serve you."..while she wallows in her rivers of pity..

Projecting perfection, as rejecting me. I, who has comforted her, by your leave, as she died. For indeed, she may have died, if not, I love you so. Now, she has sought to abandon me. I am a slave to one. I worship one. Though, I have seen gentle twinkles soothe my dark sky, I cannot lie. It is thee I yet crave. That Celestial being, you. That keeper of all I adore; all I'd hoped for. Not you, but you.

I pray you hear my call from within his very arrogance, that would render you the same portion. He who beckons you and keeps you from me when you would have me. Or am I deceived? Do you live within him or are you him?

I cannot endure it any longer. I must know. I shall not endure these symphonies with another, having not tasted you. Wilt thou force me from this physical realm so displeased? Shall we touch, if only in indecency, when what is decent about limitations? I won't be rational with you.

O, let it be calm and comforting as the pale blue sky, as you, the Sun, assume your rightful place at Knowledge and Wisdom. Love, Hell or Right; 12 our place of meeting. Let it be settled in our hearts and minds, that we might bear witness.

The splendor of the garden, where we shall meet is one of wet fragrance. God, disrobe me here and behold my benevolence. Lie heaven at your fingertips. Let me be Her. She that you have born in 7 days, I-Self, your wisdom, water that beckons.

If only you would allow me to love you that reclines behind the screen of you.

Tears

Last night, I cried tears for you, straight from the heart..bitter, sweet salty.
These tears that I have cried, have washed away my sins..cleansed me..free.
The world no longer owns me, I own it..I am it..and so are you.
Pity me no more, sweet rose, how your smell invaginates me, birthing me.
I shall die no more.
I licked the salt from said tears, as I felt my soul float,
cruising, soaring over everything and everyone.
You have born me, I shall die no more.
Loving you has indeed produced calmness, beauty, cream; magic, flowing through my heart.
I feel its touch around my neck, wrapping itself around me.
It's all in the air, our love is. Peering closer, seeing Gold, beautiful, deep and dark...
Endless, so soft, its sacredness, its serene; gentleness.
Leaning forward, I try and grasp it, disappearing in my hand,
it liquefies and curses in my blood, traveling through my veins,
planting tulips and sunflowers within those very arteries.
I have been born, never to die again.
I wrap my wondering eyes around these tears, encasing them in this cave.
I long to see something amidst this great darkness.
I only see thoughts of you.
I reach out to grasp them, but they liquefy,
cursing yet, over my naked body...rain.
Spilled illusions and false conclusions.
Warmth envelops me, freeing me.
I gently lick the remaining tears from my lips.
I taste you; delicious.
Salt.
This liquid, I have digested, shall never evaporate..it impregnates.

It lives, as do I in the sea of the universe, it travels.
It belongs to the Oceans and to the Sea..I belong to you; you belong to me.
Severed now, we are yet one.
Some far off day..some call it Armageddon, the last day; the day of judgment.
The day the universe unites itself.
She shall take forth her waters, every drip..
..and as every drip of water finds itself, again one; Per-Ankh.
I shall be there with you.
Born, Never to die again.

Surrender, I

Through the doubts, tears and cries, in the end, Surrender, I.
I want to beg you, but I was taught to die on my feet.
Upon my knees, you'd still flee from me.
Realistically, we could never be.
Something about her, nothing about me.
My nemesis has erected her fortress within you..
Overwhelming this seems, akin to war.
Surrender now, for I know when the time comes.
You have fed me scraps from her table, shavings and crumbs.
No plans and schemes have I up my sleeves.
No land mines, booby traps, nor conspiracies for enemies.

Only memories of what so resembled victory.
You'd call for me, stall for me; you'd get with me, kick it with me.
Contemporarily however, I am on your last nerve.
No lingerie can I wear, no veggie dish can I serve.
No curing herb, convincing word??
I'll give you what you deserve.
Surrender, I...
with watery eyes and broken promises, failed attempts,
contempt never pimped.
Back up the attempts at harming me with mental armory.
This war will not be won by default, theft, nor larceny.
The true player folds or takes calculated risks.
Yet at this? No Chardonnay sips, park walks, solar trips..hollow
tipped.
Surrender, I; for I have just been defeated.
Forced to fight a cold war that has just completed.
My forces have retreated, I tie the white scarf and let it wave.
Till tomorrow when I fold it and drop it for brighter days.

"Ev'rybody, Meet Sissa Doe!!"

Assaulted by the silence of loneliness, which bounces off the wall like a ball of tragedy. The straight jacket I wear seems to draw tighter, squeezing the life out of me. Its restraint of my arms stagnates the progress of my happiness. The nappiness of my new growth's unkempt dwellings bears witness that I am down and out.

It was the Fourth of July and we were all there at my grandma's house. I was simple as I could be, hair pulled back, jogging pants, and tennis shoes. I was searching for something to heal my wounds. I no longer missed Rodney, I missed myself. I was happy once.

He wasn't all that attractive, but-his words were beautiful. So meek, so humble and strong. He confirmed the fact that all my past loves had done me wrong. Didn't I know that Jesus died for me? Hung himself on Calvary. The passenger seat of his maroon Nova was my chariot and it was taking me to heaven no less. In the dilapidated church we walked, as he talked:

"Ev'rybody, Meet Sissa Doe!!"

his words soothed me, the music moved me. His beloved wife, I was soon to be. Wife! Oh Gracious God, not a wife! I almost have to be carried away, Wow!

"I say I's Married now!!"

All of Satan's demons took flight. With each scripture, he painted a picture. His eyes baptized his lies, so well disguised. I'll never tell anyone, but all the while he worshiped the Lord, Jesus, I secretly worshiped him. He was a most beautiful gem.

Till it was my turn to read.

The blood of Jesus? I'm not a vampire..hold up, if this is the truth you tell, he died for my sins, why did I just leave hell?

Explain to me..teach me..but all he could do was continue to preach to me. Forcing me to secretly discover the true the deception. I couldn't' trust Jesus, because of his complexion.

"You are Jesus!" I told him. I tried to mold him. Then it got to the part where he wouldn't let me hold him.

Maybe he didn't, but I had flashbacks of a man, who resembled his Jesus, raping my mother in on a tattered mattress, while I munched on a sour apple, saw a worm grow into a snake, flashbacks, Eve, knowledge, sperm. I remember him beating us, he hung my brother. Strangely, this was not my life, or was it?

To his Jesus, I didn't hold a torch. So there I was excommunicated, baby and bags, crying cold on his porch.

"Harlot!" he screamed. "Jezebel!"

Jezebel worshiped the Sun, Oh well.

Face Down

In the hour of my greatest humility,
In search for tranquility,
to stop me from feeling guilty,
I was face down.

Throughout all my years of learning,
I found my soul yearning,
to abandon this burning,
I was face down.

When all of my friends ran from me,
and all of my money abandoned me,
Wondering what my plan would be,
I was face down.

My heart under attack.
Time for me to face the facts.
Get this demon off my back,
Lord, I'm face down.

When nobody else would hear me,
They didn't wanna be near me,
Looking for the lord to steer me,
I'm face down.

Under every kind of stress,
Sick and tired of all this mess,
Give me strength over this weak flesh,
Lord, I'm face down.

Lord, asking for your help,
and not in the form of wealth,
I just want to like myself.

I'm face down.

Searching for a peace of mind.
Putting all my sins behind.
Lord, unleash this veil, I'm blind.
And I'm face down.

Looking for something that's true.
They don't know me like you do.
I put all my faith in you.
Right now Lord, Blessed Jesus, I'm face down, Father.

How Blessed I Am

Reflecting on how blessed I am.
Thankful nobody ever read for me.
I was just placed on a crippled bike to see
visions of a dead end destiny.
From an unstable balcony.
Nothing existed out of a 12 block span.
Still, I was so blessed to worship a superman.
Down the hall..Simultaneous orgies.
And master's degrees, and chlorine.
And just outside my window,
9s peel claps.
Traps take slaps
Mcs spit raps,
Secret lovers tap.
bums take naps..and steal snacks.
A gunshot signifies the end of someone's existence.
Gun powder in someone's appendix.
Silenced witnesses.
In the trenches of repentance.
Lead in someone's leg.
Harm to someone's arm.
The literal chrome to someone's dome.
Leave me alone.
Alone I roam.
I'm so blessed.

Meditating on how blessed I am.
Grateful that Santa didn't visit me much,
and when he did, he rarely touched my gate.
My portion for Santa was hate.
I'd be the enemy who'd burn that tree.
When I found it was an illusion, it didn't phase me.
Nature affixed, what a cruel trick.

They hung my people from trees, genocide revisited.
So, I'll just send Santa a thank you note
for never replying to the vain letters I wrote.
And I really wanna thank you Santa for not leaving the milk I left,
Simply because I drank it myself.
Driver of a car that's never saw its tank full.
Nourished now, I'm yet thankful.
I'm blessed.

Cogitating on how blessed I am.
Appreciating the fact that Barbie never had a chance to talk to me.
She didn't walk with me,
so I never had a chance to see
her fallacious image of what defines beauty.
And when I did go to school with whitey, he didn't like me,
So the idea of extinguishing a race doesn't really excite me.
Blessed, I didn't witness your betrayal.
Yet blessed to have seen your tail.
And on the back of the bus, I wasn't so blessed to ride.
So I'll just nod as I watch your race commit suicide.
Seeking to intertwine
with those in my race, who are literally blind.
So blessed, they never brought a fruit basket when I was
hospitalized.
I didn't receive a certificate when I was baptized.
The doctor wasn't beaming happily when I opened my third eye.
No oracle to guide me as I was fed lies.
But neither was my mother, so I owe more to my brother.
Content that my parents have few fond memories of each other.
So blessed.

Deliberating on how blessed I am.
Indebted to America for having fed us spam.
Negative balance of all the suppressed talents.
With full knowledge of the rotation of nine planets.

Born to be appreciative for the days I did live.
Thankful for the things that you did not give.
Embracing poverty, racism, classicism,
beholding capitalism, communism, and fascism.
Possessor of so many things; so many blessings ring,
Waltzing in my mind.
I am yet blind, but in time I will find
a sublime fine as wine.
I pay the devil no mind.
I am blessed by a world so new, blue and true,
and how it loves me so, enough to show
the places I could live, but where I should not go.
I am blessed to have known shackles, mental strains.
Witnessed the expulsion of original brains,
Sawed-offs at close range.
Blessed...ironically indeed.
The brain bleed.

My Choice

Do you suggest that I am alive, when pools are swimming in my eyes?
Are you suggesting I deny, the way my spirit cries?
I realized that my pain is my God.
To whom I have submitted, quite odd.
Pain has reached in and has guided my course.
I've known its truth, I've faced its source.
It has not remorse, only replays and reviews,
of times where I am confused and abused.
Seemed I never get to choose,
But I'm chosen.

Don't think for one minute that I am not a liar.
My soul eternally tastes burning fire, after fire.
Channeling through hard wires, my smile is bound to expire,
being that my license to employ it has been revoked.
I heard the trigger being pulled, felt the bang, now the smoke.
The lie in your voice, I discerned through the syllables.
Still I let you pump me full, it's pitiful.
So your lies have become my new God.
As you utter it, I x-ray it, see the truth, and still nod.
Admitting those, your lies are irrelevant.
I decipher the lie while you are telling it.
Still my soul submits, I play the nitwit,
in hope of what I might get, or might not get.
I'm sick of it. I've chosen this.

Please abandon me, I cried.
Jerk this thing, breath, from me, I have died.
My power is seeping, I know you are creeping.
I'm tossing and turning, and steadily sleeping.
I don't want to be considered as lazy.
My soul fatigues, vision's hazy.

I simply see that tiny part of you as peace within.
Still, I cannot fathom going through this again.
Do it, you too, are its slave.
You too wear the stains of a Queen betrayed.
One day it will haunt you, its spirit will taunt you.
As a beloved pet, the devil will flaunt you.

You will call out to me, but I will be beyond your call.
For without me, you are destined to fall.
Call for me now, while I'm listening
with an auditorial, primordial perception, which supersedes
the capacity of any man-made instrument.
Still you don't utter a vowel. You have my consent.
I yet ring your heart, as if a phone, yearning your true voice.
Your soul rejects message after message, but this is my choice.

Dear God,

As my tears block my vision, to where I can hardly see.
I need your amazing grace to shine down on me. My heart is weary, and my spirits are low. Only you can send away my pain, forever in the wind to blow. God, the pain is heavy, and I can endure it no more. A touch from your healing hands is what my soul longs for.

If only I were one of the smiling ones.
If only I were one of the happy ones.
If only I were a senseless fool.
If only I were a thoughtless bum.

Then maybe I could carry this heart of mine.
Then maybe my tears would freeze like Aspen pines.
But, I'm a pain filled sister.
God, who else can I call on?
Bless me, God..don't leave me alone.

Eternally at your mercy.

"Assalaamualaikum, My Sister!"

You tell me how I ended up in someone's college. I was probably seeking wealth or true knowledge. However, somehow within all this, I was inclined to bear witness to the fact that there was no other God, but Allah and Muhammad was his prophet.

"Assalaamualaikum, my sister!"

I blushed. "A religion for us and by us?!??

"That's right, my sister! And Jesus was merely a prophet with hair like wool and brass feet..."

"Brother, stop it!"

This man had to be the big brother of Jesus. Everything he uttered, I repeated. I was so versed. Mastering and witnessing all truth, for the unprecedented span..of exactly 1,460 days. I loved that man.

A chaste muminah, I was for the duration of his sentence. If I even considered leaving.I repented.

Why had my God, Allah; incarcerated me, when I was innocent of his crimes? Although I had my own crimes, I was a wayfarer in the hell of the world, waiting to taste the nectar of life after death; heaven. I patiently awaited the spell in which I would recline on pillowy soft couches with rivers that flowed beneath.

Oblivious and confined, with an entrapped mind, I saw it all; everyone else was so blind, and beneath me, not worthy of his grace, his majesty and mercy, which was translated to me in the form of a man..mummified in white, on a crack pipe.

This man, who was once free, or was he? Either way, now he was behind steel pillars of injustice. From behind those bars, he incarcerated my fate. I prayed for relief, the only response was wait.

As this acidic, cancerous lonesomeness literally deteriorated the very fabric of my being to the bone, it extracted protons of hope and tranquility from the nucleus of my mental cortex.

Alas, this dark sky was not riddled with stars spread about.

In fact, even the moon had become niggardly with its light. These nights were driven by Iblis, abyss...the darkest of purples, bruised, from the having not of his love. This tragedy raped my soul, as that Jesus did my mother. It taunted me and teased me. Foolishly and irrationally, I awaited his return, allowing my whole being to be incarcerated.

I would call to him: "AlllaaahhhuAkbar! Where forth art thou????"

Let it happen now!

Peace Now.

My God

Eureka, it's so good to see you again, after all these years.

I feel exactly the same way girl, it's good to see you too.

So, tell me, what have you been doing with yourself lately?
Is there a new guy in your life?

There certainly is. How about yourself?

Yes there is.

Girl, tell me all about him.

Well to some it may seem strange, so I won't say his name,
but my loyalty to him will always remain the same.
I was in pain, when he came.
From that day forth, I have felt no shame.

Well that's good!
Cause since I've met my guy I've been overjoyed.
Believe me, he has filled every void,
every crack and every crevice that was in my world.
He's turned me into a regular ole church girl.

My man is more than a man, and in my life he provides
a sanctity, a shelter, somewhere I can hide.
I worship him humbly five times a day.
He's given me courage now I'm strong in a respectable way.
It feels so good; I have a sense of womanhood.
I'm pursuing the dreams I never thought I would.
The feelings I feel now about life itself,
have never felt to right, my heart could just melt.
I'm overwhelmed with peace. I'm absorbed in care and love.

Finally I feel a connection from up above.

Well I guess you can say mine has an unselfish love.
He's not a choosy lover and he's not into drugs.
His son died for me, on Calvary,
So for now and always I will be free.
He's tender and caring and as long as I believe,
everything I ask for, I shall receive.
There are so many things I can add, if I go in-depth.
He's taught me to love others as I love myself.
He's taught me to giving, truthful and kind.
Every day I live, he's the head of my life.

So is mine!
That's wonderful. So when can we meet?

On the day when the ways of this world are complete.
So when can I meet yours?

On the day when the winds are unleashed from all fours.

I see. So where does your man stay?

Girl, he's right here listening to every word we say.
Where does yours reside?

He has unlimited occupancy from the east and the west side.
So, Makeda, tell me girl; What's his name?

You know it really doesn't matter, because he is one in the same.

The Shade

The shade of my lord calls out to you louder than the ahdan.
Peach and blessings calls out to you, the bosom of Allah, to lay your weeping soul on.
Confusion has plagued you to long, forced you to sing songs.
You didn't know it was wrong. It's been too long.
Now, I ask you, why not repent?
Years spent in a life of grief, confusion, apathy and wrath.
After wrath. Friends laugh. Then comes the aftermath.
A path not yet walked, a line not yet talked.
A prisoner not yet released, a victim so stalked.
The madness is tremendous, I pray Allah ends this.
Their plights must conform or I shall remain friendless.
No way to mend this. My people are defenseless.
For they do not defend themselves. Seek not to mend themselves.
Say, "oh, well", as we continue to dwell.
Hell Swells.
Lower and lower into sin's endless well.
What will it take to wake the fake?
When will your conscious break? It will take
God, Almighty God, the only God
to admit you the shade.

The shade that was made a million years ago.
Even if your parents didn't know.
Some of the wisest men won't go..So.
This shade offers cool.
Intellect for all fools.
Tools.
Rules.
Schools.

Will you? Can you? Your soul demands you.
Frequent there..repent there.

Stare deep inside your soul.
Look there. Although you may be afraid.
Taste the Shade..
Now End
Fade.

Lip Gloss

Everybody's talking, but nobody is saying nothing.
We've got so much to do, yet we end up doing nothing.
Clinton wonders do slaves deserve an apology.
An apology for 400 years of robbing me??!
Stop the lip gloss and let the truth ring clear.
You're done using our people and now you don't want us here.
An apology is for when you are sorry, for when you made a mistake.
Not for when you've instituted a modern remake.
Welfare is reformed, but our lives are still torn.
Sir, what planet do you think we're on??
Do you think we don't see the reinstitution
of a pro-white society? I'm starting the revolution!
Exactly who do you think you're gaming boss?
Talk to me straight up and take off the lip gloss.

Officer, officer, you say your life is on the line,
but it's the people's lives that get taken time after time.
While you ride around in fancy cars, like drug dealers
Overseeing your public plantations, yea I feel ya.
You're scared every time you take a call; you wonder will it be your last.
But every time I watch the news, you are killings brothers fast.
Locking up brothers for committing proclivity crimes,
Yet you break laws as much as they do and still you do no time.
Still you expect sympathy from me; you say you do the public service,
When you come down on my people, who don't deserve it.
I see you perpetrating everyday with a billy club and a badge,
when a leather strap along with the semi-tech 9 is what you wish you had.
What's worse, you have a code of silence and protect each other.
I never thought I'd look under a white hood and see my own

brothers.
You're modern slave traders; you're cowards, fluffy soft.
Stop railroading my people and take off the lip gloss.

United States of America, I don't really care if ya.
Band me in every state, because it sharpens my character.
I'm tired of the ambiguity, stop lieing to the people.
Tell the state of confusion, in which you plan to keep them.
How can welfare not be a way of life that's right?
When they'll always be a lower class to uphold your lavish life.
Stop lieing on Justice, because I done bout had enough.
Like Michael Jackson said, they don't care about us.
They'll never be racial harmony, because your hearts are off key.
You'll never be in sync with a people like we.
Once you open your eyes and remove the veil.
You'll see that your distorted justice has tipped the scale
on equality, on righteousness and everything that's true.
Newt Gingrich and Jim Crow, I'll never trust you.
From this point on, I demand my people to look through the screen.
Stop falling for the scheme, they never say what they mean.
They'll annihilate every one of us at any cost.
Do you think they are going to tell you that?
Wipe off the Lip Gloss!

Residence

I could rest anywhere I please.
I could kick off my shoes and plant myself in any city.
Lay back and look pretty..
and just be there,
But could I be me there?

I can ride up to any mansion and say it's mine.
But can I cut that grass? Can I roll in that Royce?
Would that be my voice?
So by choice, I must live where I feel most at home.
Even if the paint is chipping and I sleep alone.
Even if the answering machine never clicks,
the dog is sick, and the draft blows out my coconut wicks.

I can plant my tree in, that thing, love.
And falsely claim it as my life,
But in retrospect am I truly his wife?
If at night our souls are adrift..
Is marriage truly defined by who you sleep with?
While if in and out of that bed, you are yet in a deep slumber.
Is this, love, my resting place, I wonder.

I think I'll move the streets of truth.
Flex the torch of knowledge and guide the youth.
Yea, living here is bliss.
You can't tell me nothing, I got this.
I have read that book, I have taken those notes.
No pork, no government marriage, I don't vote.
A latitudinarian, vegetarian;
Librarian, humanitarian, moturarian.
Still, alas, the sheriff's at my door,
telling me I can't reside at the truth no more.
Said my truth has long been spent.

He gives me a million books and says I can't pay the rent.

I can live anywhere I wanna live.
I can be where ever I wanna be,
but can I be me?

Lo and behold, I am in the 50-Story, putting clients on hold.
Still soul is sold, blood is cold, conscious froze.
I'm on the stage naked, yet clothed in the lies of my gyration.
I'm second Lieutenant, but I detest this nation.
I'm the perjured witness on stand, gym teacher with chalk in hand,
The philosopher, who knows not a lesson plan.
The assassin who fears spice, veggie, who hates rice.
The gourmet chef, who can't spell spice.
I live here, but my heart is crying.
So I don't live here,
the fact is, I'm dying.

"Peace Queen, What's the Science?"

Peace,
I cee today's Supreme Mathematics as Build/Destroy. I see building as synonymous with destroying. Within one's cipher, their being a set numerical value placed on the number of brain cells being exercised during a given period. I see the destroying of negativity as the building of positivity. The eradication of darkness lies, bringing about the illuminance of truth. In retrospect, to destroy potentially positive matter is to build negative matter. Matter being knowledge expressed through observation, experimentation, what have you. Build is to add/Destroy, take away.
Today's Supreme Alphabets He/Her, which both born Culture. Indeed we Kings and Queens must manifest the art of constantly building positively within our cipher, our culture being Islam, I-God, or I-Earth.
Build borns Understanding, which is the best part. To Understand is to Wisdom your Knowledge, to act upon that which you are certain of. The more you act on what you know, the more you build or add to a peace cipher. Understanding is Symbolic for the child, who when produced, does what? Builds the Nation. The more you cee with your third eye, the more you knowledge the devil for what he is, A lie.

Destroy borns God, hence upon destroying all devilishment, there is nothing left to manifest, but God. God is the original Black Man with Knowledge of Self. Indeed, upon fatting your cipher with knowledge, that which you know, the devil will be destroyed physical or mentally.

The devil put fear in him when he was a little boy. In other words, the devil filled his brain cells with fear of the devil, his atrocities. However upon evicting the malnutrition of bad foods from his

mind, by injecting sound and righteous food that loves him, the devil and his false religions will be destroyed. Leaving him utterly subjected to the 6,000,000 million square miles of the planet earth on which he belongs. Hence his justice being brought about for the world to see. His due measurement: extinction.

Peace,
Queen NaAsia

Queen NaAsia: The Borning of A Righteous Name

Thenceforth from chaos spawns peace.
As from most pleasure, the result is sometimes grief.
Inadvertent articulation will not severe this nation.
In accordance with the proclamation, I submit this gestation
of my attribute from aforetime.
Hereby stating that I'm NaAsia Divine
Eternal Earth sublime.
With that being said, let all bear witness, as I present this
exposition,
Detailing the elements that summate this composition:

I-Self, NaAsia Divine Eternal Earth,
Cultivator of seeds, esteemed author of great works.
Now Allah's Asia is indeed divine.
Eternal, lasting till the end of time,
Of which there is no end.
Earth of fine minerals, jewels within.
Na, the chemically reactive element Sodium.
She, who teaches class, standing behind a podium.
Sodium, that most essential, resemblance of salt.
Master in the Art of Education, not bought,
but fulfilled, divinity unconcealed.
She with God-like traits, sporadically revealed.
Hence, the provider, protector, compassionate.
Maintainer, beneficent, non-procrastinant.
Flow conductor, symphonic eruptor, class instructor.
Knowledging the 1-14, knowledge, know ledging the culture.
Not stagnated, without a guide.
Wisdom seeds, lonely hard stride, smooth steady glide.
NaAsia, which borns born, unlimited.
Divine, which borns born, precisely represented.
Eternal, which borns understanding, sufficient, word bond.
Earth, fertile soil from which 7 is spawned.

NaAsia, the Anastasia; Malaysian Asian.
The stigmatic ecclesiastic, rhyme acrobatic, charismatic Asiatic.
Electromagnetic, Eighty-jive repellent.
Mentally off the Richter, swift deliver the mental picture.
Keeping the rest safe and warm
In this magnificent year that I make my Wisdom Born.
Hence 29,000,000 sq miles of useful land,
23,000,000 of which is used by the Original man.
Why? Because true Wisdom Understands.
On the other hand, Why does my Uncle love the devil?
Cause the wrong food was fed to him, so it altered his level.
Today's Mathematics: Wisdom Build.
I cee that as borning a complete cipher, which yields,
Knowledge My Skills.

Earth Indeed

I owe the nation a gestation of verbal articulation.
This day the flow starts. I feel the smart injected like venom into my heart.
Recently a God asked me why was I earth, and at first,
I thought Yo, I should be drug in a hearse, but as he and I versed things became clearer.
Heaven felt nearer, no longer was I the speaker, I was the hearer.
Who heard things so absurd, nouns and adverbs.
All I could do was nod my head and say "Indeed Allah, word."
So why am I Earth?
Cause I didn't bomb first, or did I?
Peace Sun, within I.
When in his absence, I practice abstinence, in fragments.
Knowledge is born through my womb or my mental.
Nor is it coincidental that I am 3/4ths covered at all times.
Making me that perpetual dime.

But why am I Earth?

I am Earth, because that's how I was manifested, wise.
I have come to realize, that it's deeper than the strength within my eyes,
bliss between my thighs, truth within my lies, sadness as my people die.
Something about my essence, because in my noble presence,
cream becomes life, darkness becomes light, word bond, I'm wife.
Bring from the left what's right, and what you perceive as nights are from my revolve.
I problem solve, when I get involved with the build.
Only for the Sun I yield, and spin at that terrific speed..so surreal.
So how does that make me feel? Like a heavenly body
within a heavenly universe, with a Divine head that's never dead.

A producer, cultivator, not quite the originator, but from the original, intercepting his signals.
Conducting spiritual telepathy with he,
Who be at that state of majesty that he can attract me with his magnetism.
She, who practices not spookism, but upholds realism.
Density and the propensity to not only produce, but cultivate the youth, with Islam.

I would say I'm the bomb, that quakes, shakes and takes mental breaks
from snakes who come in the depiction of he.
Knowing an original, the grafted can never be.

93,000,000 miles from the sun, because I born understanding
and even that three can become one,
if he is male, but he'll never weight six sextillion tons.

But does that make me earth?

Could it be because I am the 2 within 3, the her within he, the zag within zig, with the belly often big, grafting perm out my wig, ya dig?
Or it is the refinement, the logical consignment of the Black man being a hell of a God, the devil being hella odd.
The purest particle of Allah, the she, who blinds when saw, leaving them in awe.
The rich black soil, that rules, yet keeps it cool, and obeys the rules at Allah's schools.
She who knowledge is brought forth through in the form of what?
Many forms of Flesh, the mental conquest.
Not to suggest, but to eject, the best part, the canvas of Allah's art.
Indeed his ways and actions upon me, through she; manifest destiny.
Why? Because I receive the light and reflect it with all my might.

Am I Earth?
What else could be more right?

Allah sighed when he heard my response, he being 7,
he waved his head back and forth, shaking it slow.

Then stated, "Look Earth, just say you don't know."

With that I conclude this flow.

Eternal Helpmeet

Your commandments are my eternal bliss.
Enlist and subscribe to all you prescribe,
because your vibe is so sublime.
The total unwind hence I pray verbal tithes.
Cordially, suggesting you manifest forth your aluminum
to pursue and seek the seat of Mother Oblivion.
She who waits after casting forth her bait.
Insatiates and contemplates your soldiers as they vibrate on an Axis infinance.
Not stagnated, dependent, subordinate, nor nemesis.
Witness the testimony, this upright jihad.
Love nest, you've blessed.
You being God, I attend your synagogue.
With head covered, perceiving no others, shaking the wisdom lovers.
Jezebel, heating brothers, yet melt for the sun like butter.
Eve even, no logic to believe when I have observed and witnessed perfection.
Swiftness, God in person, in pristine condition, ripping away fiction,
what's fictitious, that tricked us, enslaved..the devil's way.
Now I portray and embody all that is and represents Islam.
The true Queen soothes like cocoa butter balm.
Cause your palm, when it touches me, serenity rushes me.
Envelopes me, eternity upon eternity.
OOOoohhhWeeehhee..
The Soliloquy:
Peace, the divine keeper, sole controller of all I adore.
I am your earth, your willing garden, here to be explored.
What's more? I have yet manifested self as Venus, the planet of love
To place more enchantment in my caresses and rubs.

As you dwell in my flesh, my cipher is blessed.
In your chest, do bury and render me,
your Eternal Helpmeet on this journey.

23-1-19-21-14-7-1
For My Enlightener

Oh sapient one, my nemesis.
Committing larceny on my spirit with no witnesses.
Asclepius, thine art, insurmountable lust.
Narcissus, your actions, your plight, your deen..so just.
I feel a rush from past day's orgy of eclaircissement.
No longer abashed by the esoteric pleasure, nor time spent.
Realizing and submitting to our consanguineousness.
Appreciating the plethora thou hast blessed me with.
Our plights are now congruous, for thou hath invaginated me.
Your foes being those who alienated me.
The non-arcane vows of your desire to be more intimate
have given me motivation to be a tad bit more expedient
about being your, Aurora, Goddess of the dawn.
Together we'll perform this Arica, and that's word bond.
After this Goddess, there will be no more negative
connotations.
Only shudders and sacred utters, and volcanic ejaculations.
My love, let's consociate, hence exacerbate
this utopia of me and you, I'll reflect as you illuminate.
So sagacious you are, you give me nystagmus,
So archaic, so cavalier, with one touch we'll both bust.
How blessed art I, that my God chose me
and has performed on me, the perfect nepenthe
which expands 57.295 degrees,
A radiant radian, rich and exact, like Archimedes.
Hence, there being nothing elliptical, nor hypocritical, critical,
nor elliptical, for your rays reach your earth with a force
that's not typical.
From this lyrical orgasm causing you to swell with lust.
Erecting a labyrinth of emotions like Crete by Daedalus, as we
build in echelon,

step by step.
Many tears I have wept, in appreciation of times that you crept
in silence, non compliant to your own laws.
Consistent with flesh..so flawed.
Rendering and keeping me in constant awe.
Speechless, totally absorbed in your passion without
wandering to and fro...
Awaiting you on my balcony, like Juliet did Rome.
Whispering Divine, Divine...
Where forth art thou? Come make love to my mind.

I am A Scientist

I do not believe what you believe, I am a scientist.
There's no denying it.
You can keep your faith, I'm not buying it.
I am not convinced that Jesus was heaven sent if the followers of the Messiah were Negro fryers.
Who watched us work as they retired, who hung crosses draped in fire in our front lawns, who threatened an atomic bomb.
Tortured and executed us, stating you've been warned.
With a warning shot, what an intricate plot still they want us to share a god?
I think not!
What I have are facts, of constant attack, after flipping the scene back, I'm like, "Yo, Your god is crazy wack!!!"
Inadequacy, madness, desperation and sadness.
Why is the black man's plight so tragic?
I be she that crunches numbers, the sister who doesn't wonder.
Clearing obstacles like a plumber, as they lay in a deep slumber.
I don't agree that our plights are without hope, 12 months like 12 steps to free the dope users, wife abusers, dissecting trick knowledge and spiritual confusers. It's up to the choosers, who make the best choices, speakers, who project clear voices, millionaires, who pull over their Rolls Royces, to roll up their sleeves, face the enemies and take them head on to show the black man is strong. I see most of the media's theories as wrong.
I'm annoyed. My pet peeve is there constant meddling, Norplants, immunizations, dialysis, Ritalin.
Hence, young black scholars will have the final hour, The Statue of Liberty will unclench her book as justice is showered.
This is divine prophecy, there is no stopping we, but first we must terminate this hypocrisy.

I do not believe what you believe, I am a scientist.
There's no denying it.
You can keep your faith, I'm not buying it.
Scientifically speaking, I see melanin rejects, who have orchestrated our demise with syphilis injects.
My hypothesis, there must come a stop to this usage of siblings as protected witnesses, see what the nitwit gets is pimped. Not exempt. Upon seeing the sun, seeks redemption. Indeed the sun will give him some, simply because his pigmentation is that of melanin. However, analytically speaking, the spirits of the Egyptians are reeking, because with every lesson I teach, there's someone behind me to preach a fairy tale, a myth that's stale. False promises of heaven while existing in hell. They tell you not to worry, caravans to the cemetery. Trigger to the head, Three strikes, Very Scary.
I do not believe what you believe, I am a scientist.
There's no denying it.
You can keep your faith, I'm not buying it.

I chart data on my observations of what was once a beautiful nation, experiencing an extended menstruation. However, what seems to be a waste is not exactly waste, but indeed, it is a smile on our enemies face. It is not a secret, it's not hidden, They can't be forgiven.
Whatever uplifts our people, is eventually forbidden.
I grab you by your neck and say look again, perchance you'll see that we can win. However, my calculations show that winning doesn't come by a default. Think back to the days when we were bought, reflect on the wars that we fought, spill tears for the runaway slaves who were caught. Then runaway

yourself, hence increase your wealth. Stop fulfilling negative prophecies and do some things for self. My predictions on this stimuli are simple. Thunder, lightning, earth trembles, as we assume our rightful, angry tired and spiteful. I can flow on this idea for at least a night. Full of anger, however, I'm in the lab 7 days with a microscope, pulling tissue after tissue, picturing a Klan's rope. Wondering why do my people take sex for a joke. Why do my people pull smoke till they choke? Why do young people by Polo till broke? Why sit in class and not
note the fact that our ancestors had to die just to vote?
For the crucifix, Lucifer anointed in African hemoglobin, pure Asian tortured Malaysians. Sut Typhon, exploited Isis, Muslim Son Invasion.

I do not believe what you believe, I am a scientist.
There's no denying it.
You can keep your faith, I'm not buying it.

I submit to you that in my telescope, I see stars, I see Jupiter, Venus, Mercury, Mars. I see a nation ramp-sacked of its humanity, I see within the debris, a brighter day for you and me. I see satellites that evolve around mother earth, plotting and scheming on evacuating the corrupted planet first. I see warriors like Frederick Douglas, who were doomed from birth. I see slavery practiced before my very eyes. I see the rape of
innocent, young sisters with suppressed cries. I see the conspiracy in self mutilation. I see sexually transmitted disease, a form of modernized castration. I see factories that expose our flesh. Feet so worn from work, my sister crept in the front door, hit the couch, dead sleep five minutes after coming in the house.
"Plantation Complex". I see the red scarf, blue rag, gang lovers both dead. I see the puppet masters giggle as they play

with your head. I see overseers pull up on dope sets with no regrets, pulling oozies and tech nines, t-shirts wet, as they collect welfare checks.
I see no homework, an evil, white smirk. I see white girls
date my brothers, after their race wouldn't work. Stupid jerks. I see the police riding around on horses, with whips, I try not to trip, I pull away from the telescope, grab my water, take a sip.
Proceed to take a closer look.
I see electrons of financial chaos, funds gravitated towards our extinction. I see every day; some little baby's been slain, "What are we thinking?" I see the ghetto so artistically opposed, jugulars are so exposed, that they don't know that genocide is being fulfilled right under the nose. I see black men in blue, trying to stay true.
I ask my beautiful sisters, "How can you love a man,
who beats you? I see molecular imbalance, recycling fields
of unused talents. I see atoms of misery, surrounding a nucleus of frustration. I see the 13th Amendment as a comical interpretation of freedom.
Hence, they were joking, but I'm not playing.
I see this careless personality our youth are portraying. I see so much.
On most things I won't touch, but I see a galaxy of pain, constellations of pity.
And this phenomena occurs in every state and every city.
There are those, who plan for us to not make it far, but for me:
I want to touch those stars.
I want my people to touch those stars.

I do not believe what you believe, I am a scientist.
There's no denying it.
You can keep your faith, I'm not buying it.

"Hotep, Divine Goddesses"

....and I said to him, Amen Ra, why are you hiding??
He said I have betrayed thee, and I am ashamed.

My nephew tried to erase my existence (Hatshepsut, 18th) by
destroying the images of me..he was almost successful.
Nonetheless, I am yet melanin full.
My Sun has tried to strip me of my divinity by usurping my
power.
They know not, that he is subordinate.
They worship him.
I do not desire worship, life only.
Pregnancy is my testimony.
So I let him have his way momentarily, because verily,
he had no father to marry me.
He cannot accept the truth of that, we used to spat, till I gave
him sovereignty.
He sought to do away with me by seeking my enemies
of which there are none.
I am the ONE.
NaAsia Eternal, span beyond chaos and abroad.
They said there was a supreme being, and that his name was God.
I have no need for supremacy, I prove it with infancy.
No need to battle that, which comes from me and will again
be at one with me.
I keep these facts hidden, but his knowledge is not forbidden.
On my bosom, in my lap, is the warmest seat to sit in.
Within my womb, the endless ankh resumes.
I presume that you like the melody of my tune.
Auset or Isis, my role is priceless.
My extinction would render the universe lifeless.
The universe leaves even, and this didn't start at the garden of
Eden.

I represent life and fertility, through strife and hostility,
with strength and agility; beauty, grace and felicity.
I am the personification of Nut, in a wisdom suit.
She, who gyrates to the flute of the power she executes.
There will never be an explanation for me.
I am originally first gender, with a spirit of splendor
and Grandeur...
Still at times, my physical manifestation is unsure.
In haste I confirm your purpose.
Expediently, I ensure your role.
You are Hatshepsut, Jezebel, Sankofa, Khadijah,
Clara, Fatima, Nefertiti, Cleopatra, Nefertari,
Shamirah, Ladea, Karen, Kesha, NaAsia, Natalie,
Rayshelle, Markesha, and all of you are Essential
Spawned from the Great Dianna.
You are the triple stages
Which the Original Nation must tour again and again
to know its prosperity.
The Cipher begins and ends within your mental cortex,
that you are so reluctant to flex.
Perform the alchemy to metaphysically,
that we might submerge and ascend into the darkness (418),
Where there was and yet remains...
Chaos.

Hotep Divine Goddesses
-Ptah

Questions (Mere Suggestions)

I only ask you to consider the fact that maybe God doesn't care if you're white or black.
That maybe he doesn't care if your grip is stacked.
If you live in a shack. If you wear fat plaits.
If you were a perm or dreads, if your mother is dead, do or do not cover your head.
If you have two lovers, kill your own brothers,
of if dominions extinguish the human race by bombing each other.
Hmmm..
Maybe he isn't even a he.
Woe the powers that be.
Meaning, his son never died on Calvary.
But we damn sure hung from trees,
damn sure ate up the hypocrisy, witnessed these atrocities,
and damn sure prayed on our knees,
to a mystery,
and loved our enemies,
and were and are still at times content with grafted theories.
False illusions, misrepresentations.
Allowing the next race, a pale face, to educate our nation.
The mental gyration,
confused and abused,
but if you lose, I lose, times up..
choose.

Maybe Allah doesn't care if you reverence the prophet.
Oblivious to the wealth and how you got it.
The dope and how you shot it.
The lint in your pockets.
Maybe God thinks that's your own life to deal with,

and stop trying to concern him with it.
What a lonely place the world would be,
If all we had to depend on were we.
He..he..
...hmmmmm
Maybe the Egyptians are sick of being prostituted,
diluted down to a nation that simply wore crowns.
Maybe they had jobs too.
Maybe their clothes weren't always new.
Maybe at times the Queen's eye was black and blue.
Maybe sometimes the King caught the flu.
Maybe if we really knew, we'd stop pontificating this propaganda
like we do.
There's nothing new, so take some pride in what your own crews do.

You mean to tell me that the Roman Pope, parlaying in the Vatican is a puppet on a stage, reading that same old tired page that King James ordered to be rewritten in past days.
And they say Shakespeare wrote it,
but when they quote it, you'd swear it was heaven sent.
This is a wicked government, which neglects to note that
This manual, once encased in gold, is getting pretty old.
According to this doctrine, slaves were sold and many lies told.
Warmth so cold..it does get old.

Oh, your soul..maybe it's your mind.
Your third eye, maybe it's blind.
Your lover, maybe he's mine.
For the sake of sisterhood, I'll let you keep him this time.

Rewind it back a couple thousand millenniums, when they thought dinosaurs never existed.
Now the skeletons in the museum twisted with metal bars encased in stars.
Could it be, we define who we are?
You claim Elijah lied on the messenger, and what he said wasn't Orthodox.
So he shouldn't have diamonds in his watch, glitters in his socks?
But Michael Jackson can, or the elephant man?
I could have sworn he lifted us up and dusted us off,
but you'd rather hold that Arabian cross,
and wear that Arabian dress, and talk that Arabian talk,
and walk that Arabian talk.
What's more?
They sale pork and liquor in your neighborhood stores.
Oh my, my, my..but they are the righteous?

In this life, there's just you, yourself, and a universe, that was here first.
Do you think God really cares if you curse?
What your Lamborghini is worth?
Only concerned with this tiny Earth?
Have you checked your science books?
The universe is expansive, geometry's sick with this.
Wide stretched, its conception, no witnesses.
He'd have to be meticulous about doing the rounds,
but, oh yea, he's somewhere sitting on a throne wearing a crown,
Surrounded by fat booty cupids in spandex suits,
sitting by a big-titty woman, who gyrates to a flute.
I don't see it as cute, how we dilute, and vainly persecute
Without a document that constitutes these meaningless statutes.

Let's not forget Jesus, that glorious game you play.
The biggest fool in the universe, or so you say.
Died for our sins. I'll be glad when that story ends.
Most people really worship some foolish men.
I wish Jesus was a Jinn, because then,
It could teach you mathematics from Knowledge to Born and back again.
Karma exists, that which even Jesus can't touch.
The universe is the most precise banker, with digits you can trust.

Reborn in 3 days? Tell that to someone with Aids.
A black woman taking out braids.
A bid wiz player, who has run out of spades.
A father with no trade, a switch with no blade,
sugar with no kool-aid,
and they'll tell you, 3 days ain't all that long.
Your game ain't that strong.

The black man is so strong, has been for so long,
Committee of atrocious rights, and horrendous wrongs.
His song is long, it's gripping. Stop tripping,
and clipping the limits like fallopian tubes.
Doesn't matter is you 7, Sunni, or dude.
Gangsta, stunna, or another, you still my brother and I love ya..
Cease this self righteousness, these false interpretations,
the miscommunication,
the vocal demonstration of nothingness.
Suffering, while waiting for the pie in the sky; the big "pow-wow".
I tell you, sistas and brothas, we can have it here and now.
That pie in the sky that they tell us to slice, is being digested and tested by Bill's wife.

That wonderful life, with rivers that flow beneath, is being swam in
and danced on...
Take a PEACE!

Sunburn

Into the sun I glared to find clarity.
It burned my eyes, but truth was staring there at me.
My opponent cannot stand this sun, its burn.
I've grown accustomed to its iridescence, I learn.
I allow its rays to permeate my mental cortex.
Homes wrecked, casual sex, tyrants flex.
The closer I look, the more I am certain.
It's ultraviolet rays, honesty preserving.
What was hidden lies before me, open atrocities saturate my memory.
I want to communicate this tragedy, but no one hears me.
Distilling, I, cry crocodile tears.
Instilling lies, incarceration for years.
Hence, the sun not freed me; it has placed me in bondage.
To Nun, Ra, Ptah, and Sut, I pay homage.
Take this cup from me, Oh Lords, Great 1s.
This melanin coffee cup, these revelations, this scorching sun.

Without umbrella, I am forced to taste this rain.
Witnessing the crucifixion, experiencing disdain.
This pain, I cannot stomach, I am then forced to my divinity.
Drops of molestation, pools of hostility.
The misery drenches me, my hairdo fell, I face hell.
Prison Cells, slave boats sailed, bottomless, empty wells.
Then comes the lightning, so frightening, Its plague, few listeners.
Thunderous cracks, all fled, few willing witnesses.
Lifeless, soaked, lying on a tumultuous highway.

Cars sped by, no destiny, to my dismay.
The rain turns to sleet, hail even.
It's cold and polluted from an ozone layer leaving.
And everybody's believing that which they shouldn't,
And not knowing that which they should.
I allow the rain to flood my garden. Rain for flowers is good.

Volcanic ruptures of data assault what I saw as a happy home.
To touch this lava singes to the bone.
Alone, running, a catharsis of a troubled earth.
Purgation of a sacred nation. Gestation of a liberation.
Emancipation of generation, deceived.
This glistening, great lava, which frees.
The devil cannot taste the sun's grace; he's a false being, who is only fair seeming.
To feel false warmth from the sun, you see saunas and tanners beaming.
I have the capacity to swim painless in this lava, it being my kin.
Though this eruption convulses, destructive hypnosis, it's my friend.

Within the arms of Mother Nature lies your and my answer.
End Aids, pure shade, reassume royalty, cure cancer.
The sun yet channels within me, I see clearer.
The rain ruins my garments, cleanses my soul, I pull nearer.
I am one with the eternal universe.
Untainted, perfected,
unconfined, no longer blind
unrestrained, unchained,
nor insane.
Born Again...The Rebirth

Me

On this April, 21, 2001, A Saturday; 12:30 pm....

I hereby declare, well aware, I swear that today is my day. The day I come to grips with myself, the day I awaken from the long night I slept. Incarcerated. Frustrated. That was nine o'clock, but since I've placed my feet on Plymouth Rock, I am determined to build for ME, free ME, please ME, be ME, There's nothing more I can totally be.

Ironically, other physicals other than my own can leave me totally alone. Selfish, I. Wealthy I. Stable, Faithful. Able. Free of Needs..Goddess of Greed. It's ok to LOVE ME. It's divine to be ME.

I am my best companion. The all loyal never changing hand, which hugs completely. I wrap about myself, an abundance of wealth. Alone, I take steps. The Ka, the ba. The Moon, Sun, and star, all in my conception, so they are my creation. I hereby eject every sin and abomination, I admitted in a close proximity to my elegance. Regardless of its so called relevance, if it's not a friend to me, I'm repelling it, if it's a dream to me, I'm excelling it.

And so..call me selfish, call me stingy, greedy. You won't call me foolish, and you won't call me needy. For everything I could ever need. I hold full control over. I legislate all measures, I'm covered. Anointed, self-appointed, administrator of ME! This, no one else could ever be.

So from this day forward, I'll take all this in, deciding if I want to blend. From now on, I decide based on my own

circumstances, my own choices, my own wants, my various voices. The Symphonic Concert Chorale of being Alive to thrive. Born to Grow and know, and flow to my own speed, fast or slow. This is the LIFE, not being Mother, Teacher, Friend, or Wife.
But being Awake, Aware, and Awoken, and living in accord with every
word I have just spoken. Heaven's here. In the land of the primordial, I recline. Unshackled, with a clear conscious mind, that I have just chose to define. ON THE DOTTED LINE.. I sign.....

I NaAsia Eternal Divine, hereby submit to the will of my own self. Striving for the desire in my own breast. Declaring secondary and subordinate all the rest. Hence, I am First, Hence I am Earth..hence I am ..love..I owe, I shall prove to, get used to, tell the truth to. Comfort, cradle, love and make able. Like, trust, and owe. Worship get to know. Reverence, adore, behold, explore, from every quaking, resounding shore of my totality.
Embrace my abnormalities. Witness doubts fatality in me.. I am love..
..there is nothing..no one above..

ME.

Unconquered Still

Make no mistake, I have perseverance beyond your imagination.
I've given birth a million years, I originated every nation.
Since I've stepped on Plymouth Rock, I've risen continuously.
Now we're side by side on the executive board. There's no stopping me.
How hard you tried to bring me to my knees.
You've given me bastard children and made me and your wives enemies.
Yet, as hard as you've tried, you can't keep me down.
You remain peplexingly petrified, whenever I'm around.
Do you think a welfare reform can do me harm for real?
I've been through too much already, yet I'm...
Unconquered Still.

So, you believe that you can outsmart the mother of mankind?
When will you realize, I'm the one who determines when I'm blind?
You cannot do anything unless I'm the one supporting you.
You don't know what pride feels like unless I'm the one rewarding you.
Don't you see the generations upon generations I have raised without your help?
I knitted, I sewed, I cooked, while you slept.
As hard as you try, you can't untangle the web I've spun,
You'll remain intrigued and mystified until I find another one.
Think twice before you ask me to go somewhere and chill.
I've birthed a million brothers like you already, yet I'm...
Unconquered Still.

Am I claiming to be invincible?
Dare not use such an understatement.
I claim 360 years of understanding, with no life form adjacent.
I've crossed oceans in eighteen inches of space and I did not complain.
Still gave birth to a nation within a nation, and it caused me no strain.
I've went from no voice, no vote, and no vocation.
To a vocal voter on a two week's paid vacation.
I used to be property, now I'm properly dispersing my jewels.
Using my tools, making the rules, and being no one's fool.
I was sold for hundreds of dollars now I make million dollar deals.
Through bad hair days and holidays, I'm Unconquered Still.

The Lower Branch

The tree of life produces fertile seeds.
Seeds of possibility and tragedy.
Akin to one another, sisters and brothers.
I have found you, darling, scarred seed.
You have someone landed beside me, and I shall never forsake you.
My little sister.
When it rains, it shall rain on both of us, and I shall position myself, as to catch most of those raindrops for you.
When the wind blows, I shall negotiate with that wind, beseeching it to bring me closer to you.
When it snows, I shall bury myself deeper in the soil, extracting heat from the Earth, to share with you.
And my darling, little sister,
When the sun shines, I shall turn to you, and we shall grow into the most beautiful of flowers, together, come what may, despite the circumstances of haven fallen from that great big Tree of Life.

Please visit She Hath Cried with Likes and/or Comments Via:

https://www.facebook.com/pages/She-Hath-Cried/197238186999447

www.ingramcontent.com/pod-product-compliance
Ingram Content Group UK Ltd.
Pitfield, Milton Keynes, MK11 3LW, UK
UKHW051136260726
13967UKWH00010B/3075

9 781304 987303